THE NEW FOOD GUIDE PYRAMID

Healthy Eating

by Emily K. Green

BLASTOFF! 2 READERS

BELLWETHER MEDIA · MINNEAPOLIS, MN

Note to Librarians, Teachers, and Parents:

Blastoff! Readers are carefully developed by literacy experts and combine standards-based content with developmentally appropriate text.

Level 1 provides the most support through repetition of high-frequency words, light text, predictable sentence patterns, and strong visual support.

Level 2 offers early readers a bit more challenge through varied simple sentences, increased text load, and less repetition of high-frequency words.

Level 3 advances early-fluent readers toward fluency through increased text and concept load, less reliance on visuals, longer sentences, and more literary language.

Whichever book is right for your reader, Blastoff! Readers are the perfect books to build confidence and encourage a love of reading that will last a lifetime!

This edition first published in 2007 by Bellwether Media.

No part of this publication may be reproduced in whole or in part without written permission of the publisher. For information regarding permission, write to Bellwether Media Inc., Attention: Permissions Department, Post Office Box 1C, Minnetonka, MN 55345-9998.

Library of Congress Cataloging-in-Publication Data
Green, Emily K., 1966–
   Healthy eating / by Emily K. Green.
      p. cm. — (Blastoff! readers) (New food guide pyramid)
Summary: "A basic introduction to the benefits of healthy eating. Intended for kindergarten through third grade students."
   Includes bibliographical references and index.
   ISBN-10: 1-60014-007-6 (hardcover : alk. paper)
   ISBN-13: 978-1-60014-007-5 (hardcover : alk. paper)
   1. Nutrition—Juvenile literature. I. Title. II. Series.

QP141.G754 2007
613.2—dc22   2006000411

Text copyright © 2007 by Bellwether Media.
Printed in the United States of America.

Table of Contents

Follow the **food guide pyramid** to eat right.

The Food Guide Pyramid

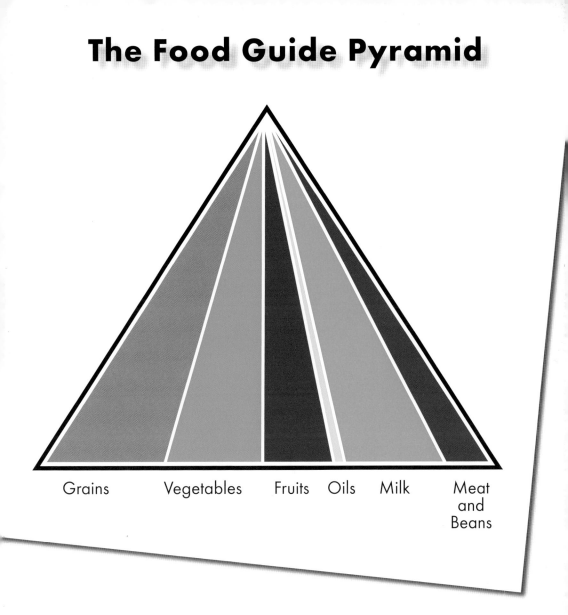

Grains   Vegetables   Fruits   Oils   Milk   Meat and Beans

Each stripe stands for a different food group.

The orange group is **grains**.
Bread is in the grains group.

Grains have **fiber** to help food move through your body.

The green group is vegetables. Peas are in the vegetables group.

Vegetables have **vitamins** to keep your eyes and skin healthy.

The red group is fruits.
Strawberries and blueberries
are in the red group.

Fruit has vitamins to help you fight colds.

The blue group is milk. Milk, yogurt, and cheese are in this group.

Milk has **calcium** to build strong bones.

The purple group is meat and beans. Eggs are in the meat and beans group.

Meat and beans have **protein** to build strong muscles.

The yellow group is **oils**.
Soft **margarine** is in
the oils group.

Oils have **fatty acids** that carry vitamins through your body.

Kids should also **exercise** for an hour each day.

Eating right and exercising
make you a winner!

How Much Should A Kid Eat Each Day?

Vegetables
2½ cups

Fruits
1½ cups

Grains
6 servings

Oils
5 teaspoons

Milk, Yogurt, and Cheese
3 cups

Meat and Beans
1-2 servings

Glossary

calcium—a part of some foods that your body needs for building strong bones and teeth

exercise—moving your body; walking, dancing, playing soccer, and climbing stairs are some good ways to exercise.

fatty acids—parts of some foods that help your kid's body and your brain grow; fatty acids are found in some oils.

fiber—the part of the plant that stays whole when it moves through your body

food guide pyramid—a chart showing the kinds and amounts of foods you should eat each day

grains—cereal plants such as wheat, rice, and corn used to make other foods

margarine—a creamy oil spread on bread or other foods

oils—fats that are used in cooking foods and salad dressings

protein—the building blocks for your bones, muscles, skin and blood

vitamins—parts of some foods that keep your body healthy

To Learn More

AT THE LIBRARY

Leedy, Loreen. *The Edible Pyramid: Good Eating Every Day.* New York: Holiday House, 1994.

Rabe, Tish. *Oh The Things You Can Do That Are Good for You: All About Staying Healthy.* New York: Random House, 2001.

Rockwell, Lizzy. *Good Enough to Eat: A Kid's Guide to Food And Nutrition.* New York: HarperCollins, 1999.

ON THE WEB

Learning more about healthy eating is as easy as 1, 2, 3.

1. Go to www.factsurfer.com

2. Enter "healthy eating" into search box.

3. Click the "Surf" button and you will see a list of related web sites.

With factsurfer.com, finding more information is just a click away.

Index

The photographs in this book are reproduced through the courtesy of: Peter Dazeley/Getty Images, front cover; David Madison, p. 4; Johner/Getty Images, p. 6; Chris Everard/Getty Images, p. 7; Andrew Thomas/Getty Images, p. 8; Wiz-Data, Inc. p. 9; Jim Mires Photography, p. 10; Julian Calder/Getty Images, p. 11; Olga Lyubkina, p. 12; Daniel Pangbourne/Getty Images, p. 13; Antonio M. Rosario/Getty Images, p. 14; Adamsmith/Getty Images, p. 15; Michael Rosenfeld/Getty Images, p. 16;   Ulrich Kerth /Getty Images, p. 17; Christopher Bissell /Getty Images, p. 18; Elyse Lewin/Getty Images, p. 19; Juan Martinez, p. 20(top); Tim McClellan, p. 20(middle, bottom), p. 21 (bottom); Michael Rosenfeld/Getty Images, p. 21(top); Olga Lyubkina, p. 21(middle).